The Smith Wigglesworth Prophecy
and the Greatest Revival of All Time

Compiled by Roberts Liardon

The Smith Wigglesworth Prophecy
ISBN: 978-1-7336062-1-9
© 2021 by Roberts Liardon

Roberts Liardon Ministries
Published by Embassy Publishing
P. O. Box 781888
Orlando, FL 32878
E-mail: info1@robertsliardon.org
www.RobertsLiardon.com

Cover and Text Design:
SimpsonProductions.net

Printed in the United States of America

Contents

Introduction

God is not through with us yet. The Pentecostal movement that began in the Azusa Street Mission in Los Angeles in 1906 and the charismatic renewal that followed in the middle of the twentieth century are still rocking our world. The final revivals of our age will be, as all other revivals, works of the Holy Spirit. God is still working through His universal Church around the world, regardless of denominational labels and personal prejudices.

The truth of the matter is, regardless of what we call ourselves as Christians, Jesus is coming back, and every day that passes brings us closer to that return. What should we be doing, and how should we be preparing, to be ready for Him?

God has never left His people without warning. While it is true that the first and best source of prophecy is God's revealed Word to us, the Bible, God has also chosen to speak to each generation of the earth through dreams and visions. This is what Peter spoke of on the day of Pentecost:

*But this is that which was spoken by the
prophet Joel; And it shall come to pass in the
last days, saith God, I will pour out of my
Spirit upon all flesh: and your sons and your
daughters shall prophesy, and your young
men shall see visions, and your old men shall
dream dreams: and on my servants and on
my handmaidens I will pour out in those days
of my Spirit; and they shall prophesy ... And it
shall come to pass, that whosoever shall call on
the name of the Lord shall be saved.*

(Acts 2:16–18, 21)

With this in mind, and because of the great
interest in the Smith Wigglesworth prophecy
that was given to David du Plessis, I decided to
put together this book. Why has this prophecy so
caught the attention of believers worldwide? After
all, this was not a prophecy given to the universal
Church, or even a simple body of believers, such
as is recorded in the first few chapters of Revelation; it was a vision given to one minister who
was then told to go and describe it to another. It
was really a personal prophecy given to one man,
David du Plessis. So, why all the interest?

There are a number of reasons, the foremost of which is the revival this vision foretold and its significance to the expansion of Christianity in the second half of the twentieth century. What Smith Wigglesworth saw in that vision was the charismatic renewal—a revival in the traditional denominations that had formerly rejected the Pentecostals and their "experience" to turn to and embrace that same experience, as thousands among them received the baptism of the Holy Spirit for themselves. The prophecy also spoke of the place of David du Plessis—who became known as "Mr. Pentecost"—in helping that revival to happen. In this light, it is easy to see that this prophecy is actually one of the most important events of Church history in the last century, as it both foretold and catalyzed what could easily be seen as the greatest move of the Holy Spirit to date.

Echoing this is the vision given to Rev. Tommy Hicks, another book in this series. This vision was not to be given to only one person, as the Wigglesworth prophecy was, but it was for the body of Christ at large. It was first shared at a meeting of the Full Gospel Business Men's

Fellowship, one of the prime movers of the charismatic renewal. By looking at and learning from Rev. Wigglesworth's prophecy to David du Plessis and how Rev. du Plessis walked it out, there is a good deal we can learn from looking at Rev. Hicks' vision about the end-times Church and walking it out in our lifetimes.

The next great move of God does not rely on receiving new words of prophecy but taking the ones we already have and living them out. As it has often been said, whether we are the last generation on the earth or not, it is our last generation to influence our world for Jesus, and we need to be in the flow of the Holy Spirit to do so. It is not time for Him to bless our plans but for us to hook up with His plans—plans that have already been blessed from the time of creation.

As we said before, God is not through with us yet—and there is still a lot He wants us to do. Do you want to be part of that plan? Then, as you read this book, be open to what He wants to teach you, and be ready to apply these truths and live just as David du Plessis and Smith Wigglesworth,—*"exceeding abundantly above all that we ask or think, according to the power that worketh in us"* (Ephesians 3:20).

1

Smith Wigglesworth and the Pentecostal Movement

When Smith Wigglesworth was born, on June 8, 1859, in the small village of Menston, Yorkshire, England, God's plans for the twentieth and twenty-first centuries were already afoot. Although the United States was on the verge of the Civil War, the Third Great Awakening was sweeping the country, renewing hunger for God and setting the stage for the Holiness Movement. At the same

Smith Wigglesworth
"The Apostle of Faith"

9

time in England, the changing climate of the
Industrial Revolution gave way to a growing
population of unemployed, homeless families.
The churches of the traditional denominations
chose to try to keep the destitute out of their
churches, but William and Catherine Booth's
Salvation Army brought revival to the streets as
they preached the gospel wherever they could. In
addition to this, in Wales, prayers were being
raised for a new awakening of the gifts of the
Holy Spirit and for God's presence to again engulf
the churches. Through these movements, barriers
were being removed between people hungry for
God's presence in their lives, and foundations
were laid for a new revelation of living by the
power of God. It was time, after centuries of taking a backseat to the doctrines of men, for the
Holy Spirit to fill God's people with all of His
gifts in manifestation.

Smith Wigglesworth's younger years were
marked by this very hunger for God, even though
his parents were not yet Christians. His grand-
mother, however, was an old-time Wesleyan, and
she always made sure, when she could, that Smith
attended meetings with her. When he was eight,

he joined in with the singing at one of these meetings, and as he began, "a clear knowledge of the new birth" came to him. He realized in that moment just what the death and resurrection of Jesus meant for him, and he embraced it with his whole heart. From that day forth, he never doubted his own salvation.

Soon, he began operating as an evangelist, which would be his life's primary focus. His first convert was his own mother. When his father realized what was happening, he started taking the family to an Episcopal church. Although his father was never born again, he enjoyed the parson, who just happened to frequent the same pub as he did, and he remained a faithful churchgoer through Smith's youth.

The Wigglesworth family was poor. At the age of six, rather than starting school, Smith got a job pulling turnips in a local field. A year later, he and one of his brothers were working in a wool mill twelve hours a day. Smith's father also worked long and hard to support his wife and three sons. Because of this, Smith did not learn to read or write until much later in his life. His desire to read the Bible was so great that he finally

11

overcame this obstacle with the guidance of his wife and the revelation of the Holy Spirit.

Smith Gets Involved with the Salvation Army

When Smith was thirteen, his family moved from Menston to Bradford, where he became deeply involved with the Wesleyan Methodist Church. Even though he couldn't read, Smith cultivated the habit of always having a copy of the New Testament with him wherever he went. Then, in 1875, when Smith was about sixteen, the Salvation Army opened a mission in Bradford, and Smith found a powerful ally in his desire to see people come to a saving knowledge of Jesus Christ. In the meetings he attended with the Salvationists, he soon learned there was great power behind prayer and fasting.

At this juncture, it is important to point out that the Salvation Army of that day was much different from the one we know today. While their work was mainly among the poor, as it is today, at that time, they saw the best thing they had to offer anyone to bring them out of poverty was

Jesus Himself. Additionally, in those early years, General Booth refused to harm anyone's dignity by giving a handout, instead insisting that people either pay a small price or work for their food and lodging. The main activity of the Salvationists at that time was not opening soup kitchens and collecting clothing but holding open-air meetings, where new converts shared their testimonies and experienced believers played instruments, sang, and preached the good news of salvation. They would even form parades led by their marching bands to usher them to meeting halls.

∾

In those early years, General Booth refused to harm anyone's dignity by giving a handout, instead insisting that people either pay a small price or work for their food and lodging.

∾

It was not uncommon for people to come to the platform, throw themselves down on the floor, and ask God to save them, while those on stage sang praises to God. Behind all of these efforts were long hours of prayer. All-night prayer meetings were common, as was fasting. They would claim fifty or a hundred souls for the next week, and then

God would bring those souls to hear the Word of God and receive salvation. Scores of people were saved through these efforts in Bradford.

At the age of seventeen, Smith met a godly man at a mill who took him in as an apprentice and taught him the plumbing trade. He also told Smith about what the Bible taught on water baptism, and soon afterwards Smith gladly obeyed and was baptized in water. During this time, he also learned more about the second coming of Christ and strongly believed that Jesus would come at the turn of the century. This made him ever more vigilant to "change the course" of everyone he met.

In 1877, at the age of nearly eighteen, Smith decided it was time to set out on his own. He went to the home of a plumber and asked for a job. When the plumber told him he had no need for any help, Smith thanked him, apologized for using his time, and turned to walk away.

Immediately, the man called him back. He said, "There is something about you that is different. I just cannot let you go."[1] At that, the man hired him on the spot.

[1] Frodsham, *Smith Wigglesworth: Apostle of Faith*, 15.

Mary Jane "Polly" Featherstone

Smith Meets Polly

Around this time, Smith also watched with great interest as a young, socially affluent woman came forward in one of the Salvation Army meetings and fell to her knees. She refused to pray with any of the workers until the speaker known as "Gypsy" Tillie Smith came and prayed with her. When they were done, the young woman jumped to her feet, threw her gloves in the air, and shouted, "Hallelujah! It is done!"

The next night, as she gave her testimony, Smith felt as if she belonged to him. As Smith later said, "It seemed as if the inspiration of God was upon her from the very first."[2] The young

---

[2] Ibid., 18–19.

woman's name was Mary Jane Featherstone,
but everyone called her "Polly." She eventually
received a commission as an officer in the Salvation Army from General William Booth. Smith
did what he could to work near her, and in the
coming years, a romance bloomed between them.

By the time Smith was twenty, the man he
worked for could not keep him busy anymore—
he just worked too efficiently! So, Smith moved
to Liverpool to find more work. There he began
to minister to the children of the city. Ragged and
hungry children came to the dock shed, where he
preached the gospel to them and did his best to
feed and clothe them from the money he made
as a plumber in the area. He also visited the hos-
pitals and ships, praying and fasting all day on
Sunday, asking God for converts. As a result, he
never saw fewer than fifty people saved each time
he ministered. He was also frequently invited by
the Salvation Army to speak at their meetings.
Though he saw great results, he was never eloquent. He often broke down and cried before the
people because of his burden for souls, and it was
this brokenness that brought people to the altar
by the hundreds.

The Smith Wigglesworth family. Front row: Ernest, Smith, Polly, and George. Back row: Alice, Seth, and Harold.

As Smith and Polly grew closer, Polly eventually faced the difficult choice between continuing with the Salvation Army and pursuing her love for Smith. There were strict regulations against officers and lower ranks having romantic relationships, and even though Smith never officially joined the Salvation Army, he was considered a private in their ranks, and Polly was an officer. So, while they would always remain true friends of the Salvationists, Polly retired from their ranks and took up mission work with the Blue Ribbon Army. Those in her Methodist Church also recognized her calling and asked her to help evangelize their churches. Hundreds were converted as a result. From the beginning, Polly had the eloquence Smith longed for but couldn't learn. Then in 1882, Smith returned to Bradford, and he and Polly wed. Polly was twenty-two years old and Smith was twenty-three.

The Bradford Street Mission Opened

Smith and Polly had a burden for a part of Bradford that had no church, so they soon opened the Bradford Street Mission and began ministering together. Polly did most of the speaking, because she was the stronger and more accomplished of the two as an orator, and Smith oversaw the needs of the rest of the work. While she preached, he was at the altar praying for more to come to Christ. Of this relationship, Smith later said, "Her work was to put down the net; mine was to land the fish. This latter is just as important as the former."[3]

In their thirty years of marriage, the Wigglesworths had five children: Alice, Seth, Harold, Ernest, and George. Before each child was born, Smith and Polly prayed over him or her, that he or she would faithfully serve God throughout life.

---

[3] Frodsham, *Smith Wigglesworth: Apostle of Faith*, 22.

The winter of 1884 was very severe in Bradford, and plumbers were in high demand. As a result, a time of intense work began for Smith that would last for the next two years, and he become literally consumed by his natural occupation. His church attendance declined, and, slowly but surely, his fire for God began to grow cold. In the light of Polly's increasing faithfulness, Smith's backsliding seemed all the more pronounced, to the point that her diligence began to wear on him. Then, one night, this came to a head, when she returned home from church a little later than usual. Smith confronted her, saying, "I am master of this house, and I am not going to have you coming home at so late an hour as this!" Polly quietly replied, "I know that you are my husband, but Christ is my Master."[4] At this, Smith forced her out the back door, then

> *The winter of 1884 was very severe in Bradford, and plumbers were in high demand. As a result, a time of intense work began for Smith that would last for the next two years, and he become literally consumed by his natural occupation.*

---

[4] Frodsham, *Smith Wigglesworth: Apostle of Faith,* 22.

closed and locked it. However, in his annoyance, he had forgotten to lock the front door, so Polly simply walked around the house and came in through the main entrance, laughing. When Smith finally saw what he had done, he caught her laughter and realized how silly he had been. Together they laughed about the matter, but to Smith it was also a revelation of how cold he had grown in the things of God. Shortly afterward, he spent ten days praying and fasting in repentance, and God gloriously restored him.

The Ground Is Laid
for the Return of Pentecost

About this same time, the National Camp Meeting Association was finding great success in the United States. American Christians were experiencing a strong knee-jerk reaction to the watering down of Scripture among academics in what was known as "higher criticism," which used human reasoning and the scientific method to throw the supernatural out of the Bible and doubted the integrity and authenticity of what was written in the Old and New testaments. The backlash came in the form of the Holiness Movement, which urged Christians to accept the Word of God as it was written and cried out for a more genuine relationship and experience with God. Within its doctrines was the belief that there was more available to Christians than just salvation— believers should not only be born again but also go on to experience sanctification, a more holy and complete dedication and cleansing of one's life to live in the ways of God. Although this movement started largely among the Methodist churches, the call to holiness and sanctification soon separated traditional Methodists and other denominationalists from those seeking a deeper and fuller experience of God, and between 1893 and 1900, no fewer than twenty-three different Holiness denominations were formed. Roughly 100,000 believers left the Methodist church to join these new churches.[5] Soon the scriptural phrase "baptism with the Holy Spirit" became commonly associated with this second work of grace, called "consecration," although it was not precisely defined.

---

[5] Durasoff, *Bright Wind of the Spirit: Pentecostalism Today,* 40–41.

A similar renewal of the gifts of the Spirit was beginning in England. On a trip to Leeds for plumbing supplies, Smith heard of a meeting where divine healing was to be ministered. He attended and was amazed at what he witnessed. What others saw as fanaticism, Smith recognized as sincere and of God. On his return to Bradford, he would search out the sick and pay for their way to attend the Leeds healing meetings. When his wife grew ill, he told her about the meetings, somewhat afraid that she would think he had finally gone off the deep end. Instead, she agreed to go to the meetings with him. When the prayer of faith was offered for her in Leeds, she received an instant manifestation of healing. They both became passionate about the message of divine healing, and their meetings began to grow, causing them to require a larger mission space. Soon they obtained a building on Bowland Street and opened the Bowland Street Mission. Across the wall behind the pulpit, they hung a large scroll that read: "I Am the Lord That Healeth Thee."[6] Not many years after this, in the early 1900s, Smith received prayer for healing of a hemorrhoid condition he had battled since childhood.

---

[6] Exodus 15:26.

After the prayer, Smith was fully persuaded that his healing was the will of God, and he stopped taking the "salts" he had taken for the problem for many years. He soon was fully healed and never had another problem with this condition for the rest of his life.

The bottle of anointing oil carried by
Smith Wigglesworth

Pentecost Returns

As the twentieth century dawned, a connection of similar incidents gave way to the return of Pentecost to earth in its fullness—a movement of which Smith would eventually become somewhat of a patriarch. In December of 1900, at the close of the first term in a Bible school in Topeka, Kansas, a young preacher named Charles Parham was leading a class in studying the book of Acts.

As he was about to go to Kansas City to preach, Parham asked his students to study the Bible for evidence of the baptism of the Holy Spirit and report their findings when he returned in three days. There were forty students in the class, and on the day he returned to hear their findings, he sat and quietly listened to what they had found. He was astonished at what he heard. While the accounts differed somewhat, all of the students seemed to agree that in every case, the best and most common evidence of the baptism of the Holy Spirit was speaking in other tongues.

That evening, the group of seventy-five people was abuzz with discussion of the book of Acts as the school held its evening Watch Night Service. The meeting seemed blanketed with a spiritual freshness. Then, one of the students, a young woman named Agnes Ozman, came to Parham and asked him to lay hands on her, that she might receive the baptism of the Holy Spirit with the evidence of speaking in tongues. Parham hesitated, since he himself did not speak in tongues, but the young woman persisted. Obedient to her faith, Parham laid hands on her and prayed. As he did, Parham said, "I had scarcely repeated three dozen sentences when a glory fell on her and a halo seemed to surround her head and face, and she began speaking in the Chinese language, and was unable to speak English for three days."[7] Soon others, including Parham, received the baptism with the evidence of speaking in tongues, and the next month, he preached his first sermon on the topic so that others would know about what God was doing.

When the school building was sold unexpectedly by its owners just before the next school year, in the fall of 1901, Parham and his family moved to Kansas City. In the next few years, he would move several times. He eventually wound up in Houston, Texas, where he again ran a school in 1905. A young African-American man attended the school there, in violation of the segregation laws of Texas at the time. The young man's humility and hunger for the Word of God so moved Parham that he let the young man sit outside of the classrooms and listen to the lessons. What the young man learned of Pentecost must have had an effect, as it was he, William Seymour, who would move to Los Angeles, California, and

---

[7] Mrs. Charles Parham, *The Life of Charles Parham*, 52–53.

open a mission on Azusa Street that would usher Pentecost back into the body of Christ throughout the next hundred years.

The Welsh Revival

Before Azusa Street, there was one more piece God placed on the earth to prepare for the Pentecostal movement to take root. It was not enough just for men and women to again be baptized with the Holy Spirit; God also wanted to see His Spirit have free reign to minister in services as He saw fit. This began in Wales. For decades, people in Wales had been calling out for revival, and in 1904, it began. That February, a young woman named Florrie Evans stood up in a meeting and declared that she loved Jesus with all of her heart. With those words, the Holy Spirit fell on the meeting, and a fresh hunger for God spread throughout the young people in the Cardiganshire area. On September 29 of that year, Reverend Seth Joshua—who

In the audience was Evan Roberts, a twenty-six-year-old hungry for God and stubborn to do nothing in ministry unless the Spirit first moved him.

had been praying for some time that God would raise up another Elisha from an ordinary person and "mantle him with power"—led a meeting where he urged the audience to call out to God, "Bend me! Bend me!" in submission to His will. In the audience was Evan Roberts, a twenty-six-year-old hungry for God and stubborn to do nothing in ministry unless the Spirit first moved him. Evan cried this out with all of his heart, and the Holy Spirit fell on him with a deep revelation of the love of God. At least one witness said that Evan fell to the ground under this power. Evan felt impressed to return to his home in Loughor and begin a series of meetings.

Those meetings began on October 31. The goal of the first meeting was to dedicate and train intercessors for the coming revival. This was successful, and soon the meetings grew to a fervor. Evan had to contact the local Bible schools to recruit more workers. The services were filled with laughing, crying, dancing, joy, and brokenness before the Lord. It was not uncommon for members of the congregation to fall to their knees in the midst of a meeting and begin praying aloud. In all things, the Holy Spirit was put first, and Evan wouldn't even rise to speak unless he felt prompted by the Spirit to do so.

In the next two years, Wales would be transformed, and more than 100,000 people would come to the Lord. Political meetings were canceled. Theatres closed for lack of attendance, as did gambling facilities and places serving alcohol. Doctrinal differences dissolved in the pursuit of God Himself, and all came together to worship and sing praises to God. Former prostitutes organized Bible studies. People began paying back long-term debts they had previously tried to ignore. Believers came from all over the world to experience what God was doing in Wales, and, as a result, the fire spread. There was no organization, set order of services, or specific location that held the revival together. Instead, it spread like wildfire based on four simple principles: 1) Confess all known sin; 2) Search out all secret and doubtful things, being sure you hold no unforgiveness in your heart; 3) Obey whatever the Holy Spirit prompts you to do; and 4) Confess the Lord Jesus openly. This hunger for God, and the presence that came with it, soon seemed to circle the globe.

The Mission at 312 Azusa Street

Hunger for God found a new home in Los Angeles when William Seymour traveled there to become an associate minister in a Nazarene Holiness church. Armed with what he had learned in Parham's school in Houston, Seymour spoke in one of his first sermons on speaking in tongues as the evidence of being baptized with the Holy Spirit. It was also his last sermon for that Nazarene congregation. He was promptly dismissed by the group as a heretic, but he found sympathetic ears elsewhere and preached in whatever home would welcome him. Black and white Americans alike gathered to hear Seymour preach, and on April 9, 1906, seven of Seymour's Baptist listeners received the Holy Spirit with the evidence of speaking in tongues. Seymour received this gift three days later, just as Parham had with his students in Kansas. In a later meeting, Jennie Moore, who later married Seymour, spoke in tongues and then walked to the piano and started playing and singing in an unknown tongue, even though she had never taken a piano lesson. Soon the numbers grew too large for any home to accommodate, and they rented a partly burned-out building in an industrial part of town. After they cleaned up the space a bit, they found that the main room—which still had sawdust on the floor from when it had been used as a stable—could hold roughly 600 people. Now they could sing and praise as loudly as they would like! The Holy Spirit fell on 312 Azusa Street like He had been unable to do in centuries, and the Pentecostal movement was born.

The Azusa Street revival would continue for the next three years in an atmosphere that must have looked much like a service in Corinth—with many of the blessings and some of the excesses that were corrected in 1 Corinthians 14—with all of the gifts of the Spirit manifesting as the Spirit willed. Conversions, baptisms, healings, and exorcisms were common. Another aspect of these meetings was that racial and denominational boundaries were ignored—all worshipped together as one in Christ. Although there were many who questioned what was happening in these services, including Parham himself, the results of these meetings were felt around the world and are still being felt today.

The Apostolic Faith Gospel Mission at 312 Azusa Street,
Los Angeles, California

Smith Meets Pentecost

Meanwhile, in England, Smith's healing ministry was growing, as was his faith. Those in the Leeds Healing Home recognized Smith's faith and asked him to speak while they were away at a convention. Smith accepted only because he felt he could get someone else to do it once he was in charge of the meeting, but all others refused, insisting they felt God wanted him to speak. Smith ministered his sermon hesitantly, but, at the close of the service, fifteen people came forward for prayer, and all of them were healed! One of them had hobbled forward on crutches and began dancing around the room without them after Smith prayed for him. He had been instantly healed! No one was more surprised by the results of his prayers than Smith himself.

Smith with his daughter, Alice, who frequently
traveled with him as he ministered

Smith with his daughter, Alice Salter,
at a camp meeting at Eureka Springs, Arkansas, in 1926

Another time, the wife of a devoted friend was facing death, and the doctors did not think she would make it through the night. Smith sought ministers to come and pray for her, but he could not find anyone willing and available, so he took a friend whom he felt offered eloquent prayers, and together they went to his friend's home. However, when he asked his eloquent friend to pray, he did not pray for her healing but for the family members who would be left behind after her passing! Smith cried out for him to stop. Then he asked the husband to pray, but his prayers were no more filled with faith than the first man's. This time, Smith cried out loudly enough to be heard in the streets: "Lord, stop him!" At that, the husband stopped, and the room fell silent. Smith then took a bottle of oil from his pocket and poured the contents over the body of the woman. At this, Smith experienced his first vision. He later described: "Suddenly the Lord Jesus appeared. I had my eyes open gazing at Him. He gave me one of those gentle smiles…. I have never lost that vision, the vision of that beautiful, soft smile."[8] A few moments after the vision vanished, the woman sat up in bed, completely healed and filled with new life. She lived on to raise a number of children and even outlive her husband.

In 1907, Pentecost had reached Sunderland, and Smith heard that people there were being baptized in the Holy Spirit and speaking in other tongues. Smith felt he had to see this for himself. He was among those who believed that sanctification and the baptism in the Holy Spirit were the same, so he felt he already had this baptism. Others warned him that the people in Sunderland were not receiving the Holy Spirit but demons instead. Other friends with whom he prayed urged him to follow his own leadings.

When Smith arrived at the meeting in Sunderland, which was being led by Vicar Alexander Boddy (who had attended some of Evan Roberts' meetings in Wales during the Welsh Revival), he was surprised at the dryness of it in contrast to the moves of the Spirit he had experienced elsewhere, especially among the Salvationists. In fact, he grew so frustrated that he interrupted the

[8] Frodsham, *Smith Wigglesworth: Apostle of Faith*, 35–36.

meeting, saying, "I have come from Bradford, and I want this experience of speaking in tongues like they had on the day of Pentecost. But I do not understand why our meetings seem to be on fire, but yours do not seem to be so."[9] Smith was so disruptive that they removed him from the building and disciplined him outside.

Something about the entire issue must have stuck with him, as he went to a local Salvation Army building to pray and seek this baptism for himself. Three times while he was praying, the power of God struck him to the floor. The Salvationists there warned him against speaking in tongues, but he was determined that if it was from God, he wanted it. However, for four days he prevailed and received nothing more.

He soon decided he needed to return to Bradford, but, before doing so, he wanted to go to Vicar's home and say good-bye. There he met Mrs. Boddy and told her he was returning home without speaking in tongues. She told him, "It is not tongues you need, but the baptism."[10] Smith asked her to lay hands on him before he left. She

---

[9] Frodsham, *Smith Wigglesworth: Apostle of Faith*, 42.
[10] Frodsham, *Smith Wigglesworth: Apostle of Faith*, 44.

agreed, prayed a simple but powerful prayer, and then walked out of the room. It was then that the fire fell, and Smith had a vision of the empty cross with Jesus exalted at the right hand of the Father. Smith opened his mouth to praise God and instantly began speaking in tongues. He knew immediately that what he had received of God now was much fuller than what he had received when praying and fasting and asking God to sanctify him.

∽

Smith opened his mouth to praise God and instantly began speaking in tongues. He knew immediately that what he had received of God now was much fuller than what he had received when praying and fasting and asking God to sanctify him.

∽

Instead of going home, Smith went to the church where Vicar Boddy was conducting the service and asked to speak. Vicar Boddy agreed. Smith then spoke as never before, and at the end of his "sermon," fifty people were baptized in the Holy Spirit and spoke in other tongues. Even the local paper, the *Sunderland Daily Echo*, picked up the story and headlined the meeting and what Smith had experienced. Smith telegraphed home about what had happened.

"That's Not My Smith!"

Upon arriving home in Bradford, Smith found a new challenge to what he had experienced. Polly met him at the door and firmly stated, "I want you to know that I am just as baptized in the Holy Spirit as you are, and I don't speak in tongues ... Sunday, you will preach for yourself, and I will see what there is in it."[11] When Sunday came, Polly did see what there was in it, as Smith preached with a power and assurance she had never heard in him before. She squirmed in her seat, thinking, *That's not my Smith, Lord. That's not my Smith!*[12] At the end of the sermon, a worker stood and said he wanted the same experience Smith had received, and when he sat back down, he missed his chair and fell to the floor! Smith's eldest son had the same experience. In a very short while, there were eleven people on the floor, laughing in the Spirit. Then, the entire congregation was absorbed in holy laughter, as God poured even more of His Spirit out upon them. In the coming weeks, hundreds in Bradford would receive the baptism in the Holy Spirit

---

[11] Ibid., 46–47.
[12] Ibid.

and speak with other tongues—one of whom was Polly. The couple soon began traveling throughout the country, answering calls to speak and minister.

This experience also caused Smith to pursue God more than ever through prayer and fasting. He answered every request he could of those asking for divine healing. Sometimes he took a train to the nearest city and then borrowed a bicycle to ride another ten miles to reach the person. Soon he had no more time for his plumbing work, so he vowed before the Lord that if he were ever again in severe need, he would return to plumbing; otherwise, he would serve as a minister for the rest of his days. The Lord made sure Smith never returned to plumbing.

Polly Goes Home to Be with the Lord

Not long after this, while waiting at a train station to leave for Scotland, Smith received word that his beloved wife, Polly, had collapsed at the Bowland Street Mission from a heart attack. He rushed to her bedside, only to discover her spirit had already departed. But Smith rebuked death, and she came back. Smith had just a short time to visit with his wife, and then he was impressed that it was time for her to go home to be with her Lord and Savior, so he released her again. Polly passed away on January 1, 1913, and it was as if her dedication and spiritual power went with her husband after that and multiplied the effects of his ministry.

Immediately, Smith started to minister again throughout the country, traveling with his daughter, Alice, and her husband, James "Jimmy" Salter. Smith continued to preach a simple gospel of "only believe." In a time when other ministers seemed frail and failing, despite the enormous revivals that had come through their ministries, Smith soon rose to prominence in Pentecostal circles because of the undeniable power in his ministry and the uncompromising stability with which he operated. It was as if Smith had no motive other than seeing Jesus glorified wherever he went, and seeing that glory kept the devil constantly on the run. He was a man moved continually by compassion from the heart of God. These convictions would never change in the next four decades, and Smith remained a growing force for God and Pentecostalism right up until his death, in 1947.

Poster announcing a revival meeting in 1934

Smith ministers the Word at
Angelus Temple in
Los Angeles, around 1929.

Smith laying hands on a sick child
at Angelus Temple. His daughter,
Alice Salter, stands to his left.

Four generations of Wigglesworths

Smith in his later years

Smith ministers in the Spirit.   Smith walking his dog on the
beach in the Hove, Brighton, area
of the United Kingdom in 1938

The Apostle of Faith
and His Worldwide Ministry

In the months following Polly's passing, Smith's fame in England grew. In 1914, he began traveling abroad to minister. By the 1920s and 1930s, no speaker in Pentecostalism was more sought after. Although he never accepted the cloak, his acknowledgment as the "Apostle of Faith" caused the Pentecostal world to look to him as one of its greatest patriarchs, even though he had never been involved in any of the revivals that started the movement. Miracles, healings, the dead being raised, and other signs and wonders followed his ministry as he continued in the uncompromising and blunt style that no one could ever emulate. Truth be told, Smith just never seemed to feel the need to be polite when chasing out sickness, disease, and other works of the devil. His sentiment was that if the Spirit were not moving, then he would move the Spirit. This was not arrogance but confidence and faith in the work God wanted done on the earth, and this attitude always marked his ministry. Smith would simply create an atmosphere of uncompromising faith in the Word of God, and the Holy Spirit would come as if He had received a personal invitation.

∽

Smith just never seemed to feel the need to be polite when chasing out sickness, disease, and other works of the devil. His sentiment was that if the Spirit were not moving, then he would move the Spirit.

∽

In 1922, Smith traveled to New Zealand and Australia, among other places, and in a few short months, he saw thousands saved and several Pentecostal churches birthed in the greatest spiritual renewals either nation had ever seen. In 1936, he traveled to South Africa and delivered the famous prophecy to David du Plessis that is the subject of this book. By this time, Smith was in his seventies and was probably the best-known Pentecostal in the world. With the weight of his ministry and faithfulness behind everything he said, Smith's words of prophecy would not only change David's life but also pave the way for his work and the greatest revival the world would ever see in the charismatic renewal.

At the funeral of a fellow minister, Smith bowed his head in the midst of a conversation and went home to be with the Lord without any pain or struggle. The date was March 12, 1947, and he was eighty-seven. While Smith never formed his own denomination or wrote a book, let alone a systematic set of doctrines and theology, his simple faith still impacts believers today. Perhaps one of the greatest examples of this is the effect of a few words and his friendship in the life and ministry of David du Plessis. Yet this was not because of any special abilities that

during my time as secretary of the AFM that Reverend Smith Wigglesworth came to visit us and speak throughout South Africa. It was wonderful to hear all the wonderful things God did through him, even though he was not a greatly educated, learned theologian but was just a simple believer. In fact, Reverend Wigglesworth never wrote a line in his whole life; he could only sign his name. His wife had taught him how to do that.

He had never learned to read, he had never been to school, and he started working as a plumber when he was a young boy. When he came to the Lord, he wanted to read the New Testament, so he sat and tried to read it with the help of his wife, and then one day, all of a sudden, it made sense to him—he could read the New Testament. He said that God had taught him how.

Now, I have met others who have experienced similar things—I knew a Russian woman here in America who couldn't read English, and the Lord taught her how to read English. She could read Russian before, but Brother Wigglesworth had never read before.

And so, when I met him, he told me that he never, ever reads anything but the Word of God—no pamphlets, nothing but the New Testament. And he said, "I think I know the New Testament from Matthew to Revelation, and I can quote it and wouldn't even make a mistake in the punctuation." He had memorized the entire New Testament. If you asked him to, he could quote chapter after chapter of it to you.

When he came to South Africa, he had wonderful meetings. Because I arranged all of his meetings throughout the country as General Secretary and attended all of them, we became very close friends. Then, when he came to Johannesburg to work in that area—the area we call the Rand, where roughly three million people live around and between, from Johannesburg center to Pretoria center, in an area of about fifty square miles—we decided he should stay with us in our home. We had a reasonably large home, not because we had such a large family, but my wife found it convenient to always keep some help with us so we had time and energy to keep the faith fight going. We didn't have boarders, and we had lots of room.

When he came, my wife was a little worried about this strange old gentleman, because if you ever saw him in action, he was a sight to behold. I have seen people try to imitate other ministers in their style, but I have never seen anyone ever try to imitate Brother Wigglesworth. The truth is, there is really no way anyone ever could! What's more, if he couldn't find a word, he made one up, but somehow everyone understood what he meant. What he liked about me was that I always understood him, and so I made a good interpreter for him. He would preach English, and I'd interpret into Afrikaans.

He stayed with us, and we found him to be the finest old gentleman to entertain. He didn't eat very much, and he always told me just what he wanted to eat. He was very nice about it. He always finished quickly, and then he'd say, "Well, you can't only feed your body. Now it is time to also feed our souls." Then he would start quoting Scripture right at the table, before you'd even finished your meal or served the dessert. He was really splendid that way, the way he emphasized God's Word in everything.

One day he said to me, "Brother, if anybody can ever catch me without a New Testament on my body, I'll give him five pounds sterling."

I said, "You always have a New Testament on your body?"

He said, "Yes."

I said, "How about when you take a shower?"

He said, "Then I lock the door." In other words, I would never catch him without a Bible in his pocket.

He carried a proper New Testament that was nice and flat. I liked it so much that I decided someday I'd get one like it—now I think I've got a half a dozen of them. He always had a New Testament like that, he always spoke from it, and he believed every word of it that he spoke. He was really an apostle of faith—the same very simple faith he always preached. There is a book of his sermons called *Ever Increasing Faith* that I think everyone should read because it will increase your faith. If you ever find a copy, buy it and read it cover to cover.

Brother Wigglesworth was a wonderful evangelist with a mighty healing ministry. I must say, I've been with healers since then—I have seen Brother Branham in action and even traveled with him for a while, I've seen the Jeffreyses in England in action among others, and I have also seen Tommy Osborn and Tommy Hicks, as well as many others. For a while, I worked with the *Voice of Healing*, and, through that experience, I met some seventy healing evangelists—good, bad, and indifferent, all kinds. I know all about it, but not one have I ever seen that had the ministry that Smith Wigglesworth had. Everybody in South Africa was interested in this strange old gentleman who knew so much, even though he had learned so little from the world. His gospel was unadulterated. He never quoted what anybody else said—because he never read what anybody said. He only quoted what God said in His Word. It's a temptation to quote these other things, you know—we need to keep the Word of God first place in such things.

Early one morning around six o'clock, he walked into our kitchen unannounced while my wife, Anna, was busy cooking breakfast. He stepped in and asked, "Where's David?" She replied, "Brother Wigglesworth, he's gone to the office already." You see, I used to get up at five, and then get ready, and by six o'clock I'd be in my office. Then, from six to nine, I would dictate all of my letters so that when the girls came in at nine o'clock, they'd have everything recorded, and they could go on with their work, and I could start my counseling sessions and consultations and other appointments. That's the way I've pretty much always regulated my life.

So, I was at the office. When Brother Wigglesworth heard this, he turned around and shouted down the passage to his son-in-law, Jimmy Salter, "Jimmy!" and Jimmy woke up and came out and said, "Yes, Dad? What's wrong?"

"Where's Compton?" Compton, one of our workers, was driving for them.

Jimmy said, "Oh, he's still asleep."

He said, "Wake him up—I must see David at once." Jimmy did, and in a little while the car left. It was twelve miles from our home to my office.

"The Wigglesworth Prophecy":
A Sermon by David du Plessis

Alice Salter (Smith's eldest daughter) and her husband,
James "Jimmy" Salter

All I remember of it was that I was sitting quietly, working at my desk, when suddenly the door flew open. I hadn't even heard any footsteps! All I knew was that, all of a sudden, that door flew open almost with a bang, and there stood Brother Wigglesworth. He walked forward, stood up straight, and commanded me, "Get up from there! Come out here!"

I stood up and immediately came over to him. He put his hands on my shoulders and pushed me up against the wall, looked straight in my eyes, and began to prophesy. I'll never forget the first words of what he said: "The Lord says,

'You have been in your Jerusalem long enough. You have to go to the uttermost parts of the earth, and He is going to send you.'"

There are a lot of things the Lord will say to you now, as if it has already happened or already exists, but, from our time frame, it is only that He intends to make it so. Brother Wigglesworth began to prophesy to me some things I knew, some that I didn't believe, some that I didn't want, and some I didn't expect to get or thought were completely out of my reach and out of my field—things that were outside of my own personal vision for my future. I had a vision that the Pentecostal movement would sweep the earth, but I thought it would pull people out of the old mainline churches, or at least that it would be a movement separate from those churches, forming a new church. But that is not what Brother Smith was telling me. He began to prophesy that I would travel more than most men

> *I'll never forget the first words of what he said: "The Lord says, 'You have been in your Jerusalem long enough. You have to go to the uttermost parts of the earth, and He is going to send you.'"*

traveled in their lives. He said, "And you will have the privilege to see and to participate in the most glorious and mightiest sweeping revival that has ever been known in Christian history. It will come through the old-line denominations"— that's what he called them. We call them now the traditional denominations or historic churches; they call us classic Pentecostals. We are classic already, we're so old. We need renewal as well.

He continued to prophesy, "It is coming in a remarkable way. Ministers will accept the truth and accept the baptism, and the churches will begin to accept this glorious enduement [or gift]." As he prophesied, he made no distinctions between any of the churches, and I thought, *Well, we haven't got anything like what he is talking about, even among the Pentecostals. This is a totally new level of revival. We've been praying for something like this, but we want it for ourselves to show everyone else how special we are—we don't really want it for everyone as he is describing now.*

In fact, he actually said that it would come through the other groups, not our own, and that I would have a part in it. He went on describing it until he finally said, "It's no use. I can't tell you any more, because there are some things that even I don't understand, and I don't know how to explain them to you. I am telling you these." Later I learned that he had seen visions of this revival that God was sending between two o'clock and four that morning.

After he had prophesied and unburdened his heart, he just bowed his head and said, "Lord, bless him." Then he turned, walked out, and closed the door.

I stood there for a moment, wondering why he hadn't discussed the vision with me, but finally I returned to my desk and sat back down, leaned my head on my hands, and began to pray, "Lord, I accept the warning about the revival to come, but if this is going to happen, I will need to be guided by You very, very clearly. No matter who the messenger is, I cannot go by what others say." Woe be to anyone who lets their life be directed by some prophet or prophetess without confirming that word with the Spirit that lives within them as well.

The Guide—the Holy Spirit—lives within us, and because He dwells in us, New Testament prophecy is not like Old Testament prophecy. In the Old Testament, the Spirit moved *upon* the prophet to speak to the people, but there was no Spirit *in* the people, so they just had to listen to the words of the prophet and obey. But today, the church is a body born of the Spirit, and the Spirit is in each of us. You can't talk to us as if we were people who don't know the Spirit. That's why every one of us has to know how to be led by the Lord for ourselves. It is our responsibility. We have to know when it is the Spirit of God speaking to us and when it is an imposter.

In the end, I don't know how long I sat there at my desk, puzzling over what had just happened, but a gentle knock at the door woke me out of my thoughts. "Come in," I said. When the door opened, there stood Smith Wigglesworth again.

"Good morning, Brother David," he greeted me, as if it was the first time he'd seen me that morning. The first time he'd entered, he didn't greet me at all, just ordered me, "Come out of there!" He didn't ask how I was or anything like that—in fact, he wasn't even gentle. Yet this time, he was very gentle. After he greeted me, he asked, "How are you?"

I answered, "Well, Brother Wigglesworth, greatly puzzled."

He said, "Why?"

I said, "Because you have been in here, you talked to me, you prophesied, you told me visions, and now you come in and greet me as if you never saw me."

He said, "The Bible says, 'The Lord said to the prophet, "Greet no man on the way."'"

"Yes," I said.

"Well, I didn't greet your wife, I didn't greet Salter, I didn't greet Compton, I didn't greet you, until I delivered the message. But now the prophet has delivered the message, and that's why I've come back to discuss it with you. What do you think of it?"

I said, "Brother Wigglesworth, I am really amazed, and I just want to ask you, have you got Scripture for such a thing?" I always like to ask for Scripture, because when I can say it is written, then I can have faith.

He said, "Yes, I have Scripture. The Lord told me what Scripture to give you: Acts 6 and 7. 'The Word of God increased and the number of disciples multiplied in Jerusalem greatly.' That's the description of the first Pentecostal church at the beginning of the church. And then afterwards, after the church had so flourished, a great company of priests were obedient to the faith." And he said, "This is what the Lord wants me to explain to you.

"First, it's a layman's movement—a fisherman's movement. But the second wave that comes becomes a clergy/priesthood movement. And after the work had been thoroughly established by the Holy Spirit in the laity and God had proved Himself, then some priests will come in, and there will be a great, tremendous move because of the priests."

After he had explained this further, he said to me, "I wish I was younger, for according to what the Lord said to me, you will see this great change. This great move of the Spirit will come round about the middle of the century"—that would be about fifteen years after we were speaking that morning in 1936—"then you will see it."

Well, the Lord warned me plenty of time in advance, didn't He? Fifteen years—and I have never forgotten. He said then, "Also remember this: you don't have to worry about doing anything at all, or seeing much of it, until I have gone home. For the Lord made it very clear to me that I must not preach this, and I must not attempt to stop anything. I must leave it alone. He will work it out, but it will not even begin while I'm alive, so I won't even see the beginnings of it. That's why I wish I was twenty years younger, so that I could see these beginnings, but you will see them."

Then he said, "Now a word of warning: God says all the things that I have told you will come to pass, and you will see them, and you will have a part in them, with only these conditions: that you remain humble and faithful. If you can remember those two things—remain humble and faithful—then God will use you in a way that no one else is used, an unusual way. It will not be the trend—it will be you and God—but you must stay humble and remain faithful."

I can see today, if you're blessed and succeed, then there is the danger of getting puffed up and being proud of your achievements. Even if you have been faithful for a long time, there is still the danger that you may compromise. However, I am happy to say that I haven't yet found a Pentecostal brother that came to hear what I have taught at any ecumenical meeting that did not admit that I was not compromising. I have never apologized for Pentecost—that's why they call me "Mr. Pentecost." I refuse to be anything but Pentecostal. I'm not Protestant, I'm not evangelical, I'm not a fundamentalist—I'm all that plus Pentecost. Don't ever stop at being a fundamentalist. Don't ever stop being an evangelical. But there is more, always more.

I learned this from a man that some might not think was even such a dedicated Christian, but I knew him as a very dedicated Christian.

Karl Barth[15] said to me, "The biggest mistake you could ever make was to think you've arrived, and stop going on." He said, "Jesus said, 'I am the way, I am the truth, and I am the life.' He is a way without a terminal. There is no end. You'll never arrive at the end—until you're in glory, and that's not even the end yet." He went on to say, "And as you move on in the way, the truth will dawn on you. You can't see the truth now that you will see as you move further on along the way, any more than you can see what's beyond the hills. As the truth dawns on you, the light grows brighter and brighter. You will think that you can stop, but you've got to keep going."

As I was still pondering what Brother Wigglesworth had prophesied, he said to me, "Have you ever been airsick?"

I said, "Sir, I've never been in the air."

He says, "Do you get seasick?"

---

[15] Karl Barth (1886–1968) was a Swiss Reformed theologian who taught in Germany and opposed Adolf Hitler before World War II. He was a founder of the Confessing Church and was best known for his move back to Scripture as the basis of religion rather than culture, science, psychology, or anything else. This concept was called neo-orthodoxy.

I said, "I've never been on the sea. I've never traveled outside of South Africa." I had been up and down, crisscross that country, and I knew every town and city in my country. I knew every Pentecostal work, movement, mission, and so on, but I'd never been out on the sea and I'd never been in the air. In those days, flying wasn't so common.

He said, "Well, you're going to fly a lot, and you will travel—more than most men, and you must not get sick. Come here!" Out I came again. He pushed me up against the wall, and now I think he finished his job—he prayed that I would never get sick when I traveled for the Lord. He told the Lord, he said, "Lord, You know it's awful to be sick at home, but it's ten times worse to be sick away from home, so don't let him ever get sick when he's working or traveling for You."

And, thank the Lord, I am not sick—I'm always well when I travel. If I'm tired at all, I get traveling again so that I can feel better. And I work hard at home. When I'm traveling, I don't have to work so hard, because I get a little more time to relax, but when I'm home, I work against time writing correspondence. In addition to that, I have lately turned my hand back to doing carpentry, which I haven't done for years, but it's good exercise. My Lord was a carpenter, you know. At the carpenter's bench down in my office, my wife put a little picture of Jesus working in the carpenter shop, and when I work around there, I'm still working for Him. It all reminds me of Him—wonderful Jesus.

After this, I didn't see Brother Wigglesworth again but a small handful of times. When he left the Rand area, he went down to Cape Town for meetings. I eventually followed him to Cape Town to help some big meetings, and right before I left for Cape Town, I got a letter from J. Roswell Flower, the General Secretary of the Assemblies of God, who passed on to be with the Lord July 23, just a few days ago.[16] He was 82. I received a lovely letter from him, inviting me to come to the United States in 1937 to be one of the speakers at the General Council of the Assemblies of God in Memphis, Tennessee.

So I came over in 1937 and then returned by way of England in 1938. There I met Brother Wigglesworth again, and I stayed with him at 70

---

[16] This was in 1970.

Victor Road in Bradford. He had lived in 70 Victor Road from the day he got married. His wife passed away in that house; his daughter, Mrs. Salter, passed away in that house; and if Jimmy is still alive, he'll pass away in that house. Seventy Victor Road—that's where I met him.

Things were beginning to happen in Europe at that time. It looked like war, and, sure enough, I found soldiers everywhere in Europe, so I soon made for home. I didn't want to be in Europe when trouble hit—it was Hitler's days, and everybody was saying, "Stalin, Hitler, Mussolini, that's the great triumvirate[17] —that's the devil's crowd—and Pope Pius." Oh brother, you should have heard them preach—why, according to them, the Lord was coming in a few years' time.

So I went home and waited. The Second World War came. The Second World War carried on and then finally ended, and in 1947, we had our first Pentecostal World Conference. Sometime shortly after that, I stopped in again to see Brother Wigglesworth. It must have been late

---

[17] "A group of three men jointly governing a realm." (William Morris, (ed.) *The American Heritage Dictionary of the English Language* [Boston: Houghton Mifflin Company, 1980], s.v., "triumvirate.")

1947 or in 1948. I had some meetings with him in England then, and again we discussed what he had told me in 1936, and again he told me some of the miracles he had seen in the vision, but I still could not really get enthused about it.

You see, the whole thing was not according to my own plans. To me, the Pentecostal World Conference seemed to be God's answer. Now that the Pentecostals were finally getting together, something was really going to happen, and we'd bury the dead old mainline churches. That was how I saw it at the time. Brother Wigglesworth said, "No, that's not it, the revival will come through the old line denominations. I don't know how you'll get in to reach them, but you'll get there. The Lord knows how." He wasn't worried.

In 1947, he died. In 1950, I made my first contacts with the historic churches. It was probably just the Lord leading me. Dr. John MacKay, who was president of the International Missionary Council, president of the United Presbyterian Church, and president of Princeton Seminary, said in a speech in New York, "The greatest blessing that has come to Christianity in this century is the Pentecostal movement."

I thought, *That's something for MacKay to say*, because when he worked in South America, he had said, "The Protestant work in South America is going on fine, except for the fly in the ointment"—and the fly was the Pentecostals. And you know what a fly does to the druggist's ointment? It makes it stink! This was the term he had used for the Pentecostals. Then he had said that the Pentecostals in South America were a fly in the ointment; now he was saying it was the greatest blessing that had come to the church in this century. So I called him to ask about this change of opinion. By this time, I was Secretary of the Pentecostal World Conference and busy working on the London conference that would be held in 1952. I asked, "Dr. MacKay, could I meet you somewhere?" He said, "Come to Princeton and have lunch with me." When I told him who I was, he said, "Yes, I've heard of you—and I'd like to talk to you. You come along."

So I went to Princeton and had lunch with him and then spent the afternoon with him. That was the beginning of my coming into what we now call the ecumenical movement. He told me that when he had gone back to South America

and seen what the Holy Spirit had done there and the Latin American countries, he concluded that if he had to make a choice between the uncouth life of the Pentecostals there and the certain death of the old formal churches, he would rather have the uncouth life of the Pentecostals.

I said, "That's wonderful."

He said, "Don't ever compromise or minimize your Pentecostal life and experience. God has established this movement." And we became fast friends.

At the time, I thought that was all there was to it, so I waited for God to make the next move. One day, Bill Wilson, whom some of you might know as the Mission Secretary for the Eastern Churches, came to my home and said, "David, the Lord has sent me through a word of prophecy that came last night in East Providence, Rhode Island. We have trouble with missionaries out on the African East Coast. The mainline denominational missions are blocking and hindering our work out there. When I prayed for a solution last night, the Lord said you can find the way to solve this problem."

I couldn't understand the Lord sending him to me. I said, "Why don't you try your evangelical contacts?"

"Try them! They rejected us. The Lord says you've got the solution."

I said, "Bill, the only solution I can think of is to talk with Dr. MacKay—he's the president of the International Missionary Council—and then perhaps he can help us in some way, and we can do something."

He said, "David, I don't know what the Lord knows that you can do, but the Lord knows you've got something you can do."

I said, "All right. Do you mind if I call on the World Council of Churches?"

"No."

I told my wife, "I am going to New York. I have contacted Dr. MacKay, and he has made an appointment for me in New York, and I'm going to New York to talk to the World Council people."

She said, "What are you going to say to them?"

I said, "I don't know; I'll see when I get there."

She said, "Well, I listened to you! All my life you've preached against these councils. Now what are you going to say?"

I said, "I might have to apologize—I might have to apologize." Oh, I was as faithful as you could find a man, but if I could, how I enjoyed reading stuff that makes these other groups and traditional denominations look bad, because I wanted them to be bad. We were the good guys; they were the bad guys. I only read the worst stuff about the Catholics, because I wanted to have an excuse to have nothing to do with them. It is easy to find an excuse to believe that the old crowd's too bad to associate with, that God is calling us to "come out from among them." Yet, if they were really as bad as we think, then we ought to go in and save them, not sit back and condemn them. Shouldn't we save bad people? Or are we only looking for good people to save? If you are looking for good people, you're looking for the other fellow's sheep, and I guarantee you'll end up with his goats. We are not called to sheep stealing; we are called to seek and save the lost.

After I decided to go, I remember praying, "Lord, You've told me to go to these people, and now this issue with Brother Wilson and the Pentecostal Missions is really giving me a good reason." So I went to New York.

When I arrived and was with them, I began to tell them about our Pentecostal missions. Of course, I had to talk about missions, since I had this situation in Kenya. Our brethren there were having difficulty because they couldn't get recognition from the Council of Churches, and the government therefore was cool on them. However, when I finished talking about the missions, the chief in the office there asked me to keep on telling him about Pentecost. When lunch came, there was finally a lull of silence. I said, "It's twelve o'clock and it's lunchtime. I'm sorry I took so much of your time."

He said, "No, you didn't take my time. I took yours, because I'm asking the questions." He asked, "You eat lunch?"

I said, "Yes."

He said, "I'll pay for it if you keep talking."

So we went to lunch, and I kept talking. When we came back, he called the office staff together, and he made me repeat to them all those things that I thought they didn't want to hear. I was sure he'd tell me to get out, but instead he kept me there. In the end, he asked me, "Where have you been all this time?"

I said, "Sir, I've only lived in America for a while. I'm a South African."

"Well, where are your Pentecostal leaders? None of them have ever come and talked to us. We can't get anyone from any Pentecostal group, anywhere, to come talk with us. How are we supposed to get ahold of these people when they always run away from us?"

I said, "Well, you call us Pentecostals 'crazy fanatics'—who wants to talk to a man that calls you a 'crazy fanatic'?"

"Yes," he said, "it may be true, but you call us 'unbelieving devils.'"

Now I said, "That's true, too, but I didn't come here to call you names."

He said, "That's why I'm not calling you names. I love to hear what you have to say. We've been waiting for a man like you."

In the end, I stayed there until four o'clock in the afternoon. When we finally finished, they asked me to write a letter to them recommending and endorsing the Pentecostal missions groups in East Africa—if I remember correctly, it was the Eagle Missionary Assemblies and some other group in Pennsylvania, and then Mrs. Gibson's people from the East Coast Zion Bible Institute. There were three groups, and I recommended and endorsed all of them. I said, "These are my brethren, and I know them to be honest, trustworthy men, and I would recommend that they get some protection or some help."

The office in New York wrote to the London office of the International Missionary Council—later on, I got acquainted with those secretaries—and they wrote to the British Colonial office in Kenya. In those days, Kenya and those eastern countries were still under British control. Not long afterwards, I learned that the British Colonial office had ordered their heads in the colonies to let these Pentecostal missions groups operate freely. Thank God for what's happened in East Africa since then.

That was the beginning of my cooperation with the ecumenical groups. They saw themselves as service groups. They said, "We are not here to control; we are here to serve." I wish every service agency that was ever established would remain a service agency, but God have mercy when service agencies become controlling agencies. That's where the trouble starts—when such groups begin to strive to control instead of serve.

I think for the rest, you know the story. In England, Brother Wigglesworth only told a few brethren that he knew there was a great revival coming. Something I left out was that, when I came here in 1937, I met Dr. Charles Price[18] in Pasadena, and we spent an afternoon together. He wanted to know all about Brother Wigglesworth. They had met, and they knew each other, but Dr. Price was a highly educated man, and Wigglesworth was an uneducated man. When they had met, Brother Wigglesworth would say, "I wish I

---

[18] Dr. Charles S. Price (1887–1947) was a great Pentecostal leader in the United States during the first half of the twentieth century who moved greatly in the gifts of healings and miracles.

could be like Charles Price," and Charles Price said to me, "I wish I had no education, and I was like Wigglesworth. Then I'd be more spiritual."

I told him then, "Brother Wigglesworth predicts that there is a tremendous revival that is going to sweep the world. The world—not some countries—but the world! And all the churches."

Dear old Charles Price just burst out in tears. "Oh," he said, "thank God, thank God. There's someone else who got the vision."

> ∾
>
> *I told him then, "Brother Wigglesworth predicts that there is a tremendous revival that is going to sweep the world. The world—not some countries—but the world! And all the churches."*
>
> ∾

I said, "You got it, too?"

He said, "Yes, but I dare not talk about it. The brethren all say to me, in the last days the love of many shall wax cold. They believe that there will be no greater revival—that we Pentecostals are the last wave."

The last wave. No wonder I once heard a Pentecostal pastor say, "God has made us the holders of the Holy Spirit—if people want Him, let them come to *us*."

How sad. You know, when I think of this, I think the Catholic Church must have been Pentecostal at some point, because when Pentecostals begin to think they are *the* church, they're just like Catholics. "Now *we* are *the* church."

I remember the battle we had in the Church of God in Cleveland, Tennessee. You know, they used to be *the* Church of God, and nobody else but they were right. There are still some of them that believe that way. Well, thank God for shaking us up—and shaking us out of the old ruts that we've gotten ourselves into.

But my point is that Dr. Price confirmed all that Brother Wigglesworth had said to me, and these two old pioneers blessed me and encouraged me so much. So, friends, gradually I've come to move easily within different church circles. It began with missions work and at the World Council of Churches headquarters, and then, in 1952, they invited me to the International Missionary Council in Germany. It was there that Dr. MacKay did something very unusual. At such conferences, they never asked visitors to speak. They usually already have a program lined up well in advance. However, one day, a Methodist missionary was telling how our mainline Christian institutions were ruining Christianity in India. Years ago, revival had hit there, and the Methodist church established a school, but today that school has only 10 percent Christian students and only 5 percent Christian teachers, even though it's still a Methodist school. He said, "The best thing that could happen to us there is that someone set fire to the place and burn it down."

At that, Dr. MacKay got up, and he said, "All right, while you fellows are burning down your institutions, I want a gentleman that's with us here to come and tell us how the Pentecostals, without institutions, have been sweeping around the world with a missionary message that is shaking the earth." In those days—that's 1952—Pentecostals weren't as strong on education as we are today. Today, you can find a doctor on every Pentecostal platform. I don't know where they get these degrees, but some of them have no more warmth than the number of degrees they have. But, back in 1952, we Pentecostals didn't think too much of such degrees. However, the same was not true among ecumenicals, so when Dr. MacKay introduced me, he called me "*Dr.* du Plessis." Somehow, after that, it stuck. After that, people kept asking me, "Where did you get your doctorate?" To that, I would always answer, "I don't have one. It was just that Dr. MacKay called me 'Doctor' at a conference once and it stuck."

"I see," they'd say. "So, you haven't got a D.D.?"

"Oh, yes, I have a D.D., a small d.d.—it stands for 'David the Donkey.'"[19] That is what I had thought in 1920 when I began to work for the Lord: "I'm the Lord's Donkey." You see, David the Donkey was my title in South Africa. People still know me by that name if you're ever in South Africa.

Well, at that missionary conference, I saw where the churches were going. They asked me, "How did the Pentecostals do it?" I said, "By everyone being a witness. Each one teach one, witnessing, being Christians, living the life." Today, we're not about just being Christians but

---

[19] David did, however, earn his own D.D. in 1978 from Bethany Bible College in Santa Cruz, California, as recognition of his life's work and teachings.

all about degrees. When churches call to find pastors, they want to know the man's educational qualifications. Missionaries have to have certain qualifications or they can't pass certain board requirements. They even make them take psychological tests. Good Lord, have mercy upon us if an ungodly psychiatrist has to make the judgment of the fitness of a Spirit-filled man and woman for the missions field—for

Missionaries have to have certain qualifications or they can't pass certain board requirements. They want clever people, but it's the foolishness of the gospel that has changed these countries, not the wisdom of men.

how could he understand? Where does he get his information? Is he getting it from ungodly psychiatrists in other countries? None of us can fit into that kind of man-devised frame, because "the natural man receiveth not the things of the Spirit."[20] They are forever foolishness to him, and they don't want to send fools out to these foreign countries. They want clever people, but it's the foolishness of the gospel that has changed these countries, not the wisdom of men.

---

[20] 1 Corinthians 2:14.

81

So today, the Lord has changed things to the point that I can hardly believe it sometimes. I am so at ease—and so happy—in all kinds of meetings, but thank God for the men and brethren that have been willing to help me in this. Once, I was supposed to go to an institute in New York and I couldn't go, so I asked Brother Spencer to go for me. Here and there, I have found brethren who are willing to go. In some cases, I've recommended Pentecostal leaders willing to go and speak at certain conferences. Yet, when they received the invitation, they absolutely refused to go.

But I never refused. I've gone if I can, even though sometimes I can't for financial reasons. Believe me, there isn't money in this kind of an outreach. If I wanted to make money, I should try to be an evangelist or something like that— you know, spend an hour raising an offering and then preach for half an hour. But I didn't go that way. However, I do believe the Lord still honors faith and obedience, and so He takes care of me.

Recently this year, I had to go to Indonesia, and I wasn't sure if God wanted me to go. Then a brother knocked at my door, came in, sat down, and shared a few wonderful Scriptures with me. When he finished, I said, "This is just what I needed to encourage me on my way to Indonesia."

"Oh yes," he said, "but the Lord also told me to give you this," and he handed me a thousand dollars. So, that takes care of it. Not only the promises, but also the blessing with it.

When I had to go to Chile, just last May, I had only two days to speak at a conference of four hundred ministers. I prayed, "Lord, I haven't got time to stay longer."

He said, "Go."

I said, "Lord, the fare is $770. You want me to spend that much for only two days?"

"I'll pay your fare."

I had a meeting in Glendale at Faith Center that Sunday morning. They had already taken up all of the offerings for the day when the pastor said, "I feel we ought to help Brother David. He's got a call to Santiago, Chile." So they took up another offering. That evening he came and gave me a check for $600—my, that was great. He said, "That's not all," and he gave me another check for $170. Together they were $770! Exactly the fare I needed for the trip.

I said, "All right, Lord. If You pay that easily, I'll travel easy," and I went. Oh, what a time I had those three days in Chile—how the Lord blessed that trip! That's the way He takes care of things. That's the way He supplies.

Tomorrow, I will preach in the Episcopal church in Selma. On Monday, I will meet the ministers, and then we will go for a few days to a camp meeting in the mountains. Then we fly to Europe. When I was in London, England, last November, the Catholics invited Brother Ray Bringham and me to a conference in Spain. The cardinal said, "Will both of you come to a Pentecostal Charismatic Catholic conference at the university in Salamanca in Spain? The invitation is with the approval of the bishop!" So we're going to have a Pentecostal conference in Spain at a Catholic university.

From there, I will be making my first renewal visit with the Vatican in Rome—not with the pope, though. I will meet with the cardinal who is president of the Secretariat for Promoting

Christian Unity, Cardinal Willebrands, and they have agreed they would now like to have dialogue with Pentecostals on September 2 and 3. So I'm going to Rome to meet with them.

Now, I know a Catholic priest who has said, "David is going to talk to the pope." I can only say, "Then that must be prophetic," because I haven't made such arrangements. However, if it happens when I get there, that would be all right. Will you pray that the Lord will help me? I have been in the Pentecostal movement now for the last fifty-two years—I received the baptism in 1918—and, my brethren, nowhere has this revival of the Holy Spirit sparked and moved as fast as it's now moving in Catholic churches. Not even in the original Pentecostal movements nor in the Protestant churches has the baptism of the Holy Spirit been received so quickly by so many.

The Spirit is moving throughout the world, and everywhere I go, I find people telling me how the Catholic priests and nuns and professors are embracing it. It really is a movement among the learned and the priests—among their educated and cultured people. Throw away those with other prophecies and all the naysayers—this revival, birthed by the Holy Spirit, is coming through, and the best of it still hasn't happened yet.

3

❧

The Wigglesworth Prophecy—
Other Sources and Information

One of the problems in researching the Smith Wigglesworth prophecy to David du Plessis is finding the exact wording of what was said on that morning in December 1936. One of the main reasons for this is, of course, that it was never recorded or written down until sometime in the early 1950s. The earliest reference to it in the writings of David du Plessis is an article that was published in 1951:

> How well I remember the increased desire for fellowship when the late Smith Wigglesworth visited South Africa in

1936. One morning early he came into my office and without a word of greeting said: "Young man, you have been in Jerusalem long enough and the Lord says that you have to go to the uttermost parts of the earth." I was dumbfounded. "He has much work for you and you will be going soon." Then he prayed: "Lord, let him always enjoy Your blessings and never get sick on his many travels ahead." Later he spoke to me and warned me that absolute obedience at all cost will be the price for having a share in the greatest wave of revival that ever has been known in history.[21]

What is most significant about this account is that it is truly before David was involved in this revival—or any of the traditional churches were involved—as this did not happen until after his first meeting with Dr. MacKay and the World Council of Churches headquarters, which, as you will remember, took place in 1952.

---

[21] David du Plessis, *By One Spirit into One Body*, 1, quoted in Robinson, "To the Ends of the Earth," 87.

Another likely reason that David had a hard time remembering the prophecy word for word was because of the nature of Brother Wigglesworth's delivery of what he had seen in his vision. David must have been somewhat in a state of shock while hearing it, as he was pinned to the wall by Smith's strong hands. Through the research of Father Peter Hocken, who has made the best attempt to date to document the original prophecy, it has been discovered that at least four different versions of this prophecy exist, all which differ slightly because of the time between the event and the writing and David's inadvertent addition of other things God had shown him through his meditations upon and walking out of the vision. According to Father Hocken's work, the four versions are found in David's autobiography, *A Man Called Mr. Pentecost* (1977), the souvenir brochure from the Third World Pentecostal Conference (1952), *As at the Beginning* (1965), and an article in *A Voice of Faith* (1964). The version in David's autobiography is the most official of these and is very similar to the one presented in his 1970 address (which appeared in the previous chapter), though it does have some additional details of what was spoken.

From putting these four versions together using a somewhat unscientific and "educated guess" system, Father Hocken came up with the following approximation of what was said to David du Plessis as he stood pinned to the wall by Smith Wigglesworth:

There is a revival coming that at present the world knows nothing about. It will come through the churches. It will come in a fresh way. When you see what God does in this revival, you will then have to admit that all you have seen previously is a mere nothing in comparison with what is to come. It will eclipse anything that has been known in history. Empty churches, empty cathedrals will be packed again with worshippers. Buildings will not be able to accommodate the multitudes. Then you will see fields of people worshipping and praising together. The Lord intends to use you in this revival. For you have been in Jerusalem long enough. The Lord will send you to the uttermost parts of the earth. If you are faithful and humble, the Lord will use you, and if you remain faithful

and humble, you will see the greatest
events in church history.[22]

While this lag in time
might lead some to doubt
the validity of this prophecy,
there is some good evidence
to corroborate it. The first is
a conversation that was had
with Smith Wigglesworth
in New Zealand:

> *There is a revival
> coming that at
> present the world
> knows nothing about.
> It will come through
> the churches. It will
> come in a fresh way.*

In the book *New Zealand's Greatest
Revival...* a brother remarked to Smith
Wigglesworth: "One is tempted to envy
you when you have had such great success."

He received the following reply: "Young
man, it is the other way around. I feel
like envying you. I have had three visions
in my life—three only. The first two have
already come to pass, but the third is yet
to be fulfilled. I will most likely pass on
to my reward, but you are a young man

---

[22] Peter Hocken, "Baptised in the Spirit: The Origins and
Early Development of the Charismatic Movement in Great
Britain" (Ph.D. Thesis, University of Birmingham, 1984), 2,
in Martin, "To the Ends of the Earth," 87.

and will most likely be in what I saw." He burst out, "Oh, it was amazing. Oh," he said, "I cannot tell God's secrets. But you remember what I say—this revival we have had is nothing to what God is yet going to do."

The one to whom Brother Wigglesworth addressed these words commented: "It was quite evident that the evangelist had a special vision granted him of the coming outpouring of the Spirit in an unprecedented effusion in the days just before our Lord comes to snatch away the church."[23]

The second is the change that was brought to the life of David du Plessis. David would have been among the last to seek ecumenical ties because he grew up fighting them throughout his early ministry. It is somewhat similar to the change that was seen in Peter on the day of Pentecost. While Peter had been a coward and denied Christ three times on the night before Jesus' crucifixion, on the day of Pentecost he stepped up before the

---

[23] Gordon Lindsay, "Are the Gifts of the Spirit for the Church Today?" *Voice of Healing* (1963), 5, in Martin, "To the Ends of the Earth," 100.

crowd and proclaimed that Jesus was the Messiah, to such effect that three thousand were saved that day. In the words of many who have looked at this situation, "Something definitely happened to inspire that change," and this is one of the evidences given time and again for the resurrection of Jesus. Something tremendous happened to make that change, and it couldn't have been the disciples stealing away Jesus' body in the dead of night, because Peter never could have come up with such conviction if he had known it was all a fraud. In the same way, we know something must have happened to David du Plessis to change his attitude toward the mainline denominations from being the enemies of Christ to being the main focus to whom Christ wanted him to reach out with love and forgiveness.

Because of these things, among others, researchers into the work of David du Plessis have not only come to the conclusion that the prophecy was genuine, but also that this prophecy was one of the most significant events of the twentieth century. It was the conception of the charismatic renewal that would bring the Pentecostal reawakening from fringe groups into the mainstream churches. While organizations, such as the Full Gospel Business Men's Fellowship, and ministries, such as Kathryn Kuhlman's, welcomed people of all denominations into their meetings and introduced them to the baptism in the Holy Spirit, David du Plessis was the one who gave doctrinal support—albeit not of a scholarly nature—to what they were doing (as to a somewhat lesser extent did Donald Gee and his writings) and was the voice to church leaders around the world that this was a move of the Spirit aligned with sound biblical interpretation. For this reason, the move was accepted rather than shut down in some of the most unexpected places, not the least of which was the Catholic Church. And, as a result, churches have filled to overflowing, and Pentecostalism has been one of the strongest missionary outreaches in the last several hundred years, including the mass revivals that began in Argentina in 1954 with Tommy Hicks and continue today in Africa in the ministry of Reinhard Bonnke.

More than this historical significance, though, is the fact that there is much to learn about prophecy—and fulfilling the prophecy of this word from Smith Wigglesworth, as well as the effect it had on the life of David du Plessis. For that reason, it is worth taking the time to look further into the gift of prophecy and how we are to apply it in our own lives when we hear a prophetic word.

4

❧

Fulfilling Prophecy

Blessed is he that readeth, and they that hear
the words of this prophecy, and keep those
things which are written therein: for the time
is at hand ... For the testimony of Jesus
is the spirit of prophecy.
—Revelation 1:3; 19:10

The ultimate purpose of all prophecy is to lift up Jesus for the salvation of all who hear. The simple test of the soundness of prophecy is this: false prophecy will puff up the person or people hearing it, feeding their egos; true prophecy will lift up Christ. Thus, Smith Wigglesworth's conditions on his prophecy to David du Plessis ring true:

God says all the things that I have told you already will come to pass, and you will see them, and you will have part in them, with only this condition, *that you remain humble and faithful.* If you can remember those two things—remain humble and faithful—then God will use you in a way that no one else is used, unusual, it will not be the trend, it will be you and God, and you must keep *humble* and remain *faithful.*[24]

The true purpose of this prophecy was not that David would have a huge international ministry—even though that is what it turned out to be—but that he would have a new way to testify of Jesus Christ among traditional churches that had all but forgotten about His true nature and the ministry of His Holy Spirit.

Echoing his teachings on prophecy which are included in the Tommy Hicks book in this series. Smith Wigglesworth establishes that there are three classes of prophecy and three purposes for it (subservient to the ultimate purpose of testifying of Jesus). In 1927, in a teaching presented to a

---

[24] The italics have been added to emphasize the point here.

group of Bible students at Angelus Temple in Los Angeles, Smith Wigglesworth identified the types of prophecy as being either 1) the testimony of a person who has been saved, 2) the words of a minister in a message spoken under the anointing of God, or 3) someone speaking out of the gift of prophecy through a vision or by the inspiration of the Holy Spirit. Considering these options, we see that Smith's prophecy

The true purpose of this prophecy was not that David would have a huge international ministry—even though that is what it turned out to be—but that he would have a new way to testify of Jesus Christ among traditional churches.

to David falls into the third category. He also stated that, according to 1 Corinthians 14:3, prophecy is for the 1) edification, 2) exhortation, and 3) consolation of the hearers. When it is used for edification, it strengthens the believers as they humble themselves before Christ and enables them to do what God has called them to do. Exhortation directs and motivates them to act— there is something they need to do, whether that is responding to the message of salvation or acting upon something God has put in their hearts to do. Under prophecy that exhorts, it is also important to recognize that prophecy also instructs and informs. Sometimes prophecy instructs us in directions we should go, giving conditional directions in a sort of "If…, then…" format. A good deal of scriptural instruction falls into this category. One example is James 4:7–8:

> *Submit yourselves therefore to God. Resist the devil, and he will flee from you. Draw nigh to God, and he will draw nigh to you.*

Would you like the devil to flee from you? Then you must a) submit yourself to God and b) resist the devil. These two conditions are necessary before you can collect the promise of Satan fleeing from you. Do you want God to draw close to you? Then you must first draw close or seek after Him. As Jeremiah 29:13 says, *"Ye shall seek me, and find me, when ye shall search for me with all your heart."* Other prophecy is unconditional and informs us of what is going to happen no matter how we act. The book of Revelation is this type of prophecy. In this light, Smith Wigglesworth's prophecy to David du Plessis was a bit of both. It was unconditional in that the revival he saw in the vision was coming no matter what people did. However, it was also conditional: if David wanted to be part of that revival, then he needed to stay humble and faithful. Thank God for all of us that he did. But, had he not, God would have found someone else to fill that role in the charismatic renewal.

Lastly, prophecy is for consolation—helping believers recover from setbacks or loss by reemphasizing God's love for them and His power to redeem them from whatever they may be facing and to bring comfort to the situation. Again, in this context, Smith Wigglesworth's prophecy to David du Plessis includes at least two of these three: edification to know that God had called him to a specific task and exhortation to act on it and stay humble and faithful so that he could accomplish it. There may also have been a note of consolation in that David would also be healed of the pains inflicted previously by the mainline denominations—specifically the Dutch Reformed ministers—and that he would be reconciled with these congregations that had initially opposed the Pentecostal movement. Of course, this was much easier to see in retrospect than in 1936, or even in 1950, when David was just embarking on what would become his part in the charismatic renewal of the 1950s, 1960s, and 1970s. It is one thing to look back and see how prophecy worked, but it is quite another to hear it and know how to act upon it. How are we to judge prophecy so that we may discern how to act upon it?

Judging Prophecy

The first rule of judging prophecy is still the best: Does the word puff up the hearer or lift up Christ? As John said in his first epistle:

> *Beloved, believe not every spirit, but try the spirits whether they are of God: because many false prophets are gone out into the world. Hereby know ye the Spirit of God: Every spirit that confesseth that Jesus Christ is come in the flesh is of God: And every spirit that confesseth not that Jesus Christ is come in the flesh is not of God: and this is that spirit of antichrist, whereof ye have heard that it should come; and even now already is it in the world.*

> (1 John 4:1–3)

Any spirit that denies either Jesus' full physical incarnation in coming to earth or His full deity as part of the Godhead is not from God. Any spirit that speaks of the greatness of the hearer to touch his ego rather than touch his spirit is not lifting up Christ and is not from God. Such are spirits that seek to deceive rather than edify, exhort, or console with the goal of bringing hearers to kneel at the foot of the cross.

A second test is whether or not the word of prophecy aligns with specific Scriptures or principles of the Bible. What was David's first question to Smith Wigglesworth when he came back after delivering this prophecy? "Brother Wigglesworth, I am really amazed, and I just want to ask you, *have you got Scripture for such a thing?*"[25] When he posed this question, Smith Wigglesworth gave him the scriptural examples of what he had seen in his vision.

> *Any spirit that denies either Jesus' full physical incarnation in coming to earth or His full deity as part of the Godhead is not from God.*

---

[25] The italics have been added for emphasis.

Just as with following Jesus, the Pentecostal movement would first be a fisherman's—or layperson's—movement among those hungriest for all that God had to give, and then it would be a priestly movement among those who had long professed God but rejected Him when they met Him face-to-face. Just as the Pharisees and Sadducees rejected Jesus because they clung to their false interpretations of the Scriptures rather than seeing the truth in His, the mainline denominations missed the Holy Spirit when He came for a renewal of Pentecost through Azusa Street and similar places. And, just as many of the priests came to Christ after His resurrection, many in the mainline denominations would accept the baptism of the Holy Spirit once they saw the fruit it had produced in the lives of other believers. No spoken prophecy that is from God will contradict the teachings of the Bible. To emphasize this further, we need to look at what Peter said in his second epistle to the churches:

> *For we have not followed cunningly devised*
> *fables, when we made known unto you the*
> *power and coming of our Lord Jesus Christ,*
> *but were eyewitnesses of his majesty. For*

he received from God the Father honour and glory, when there came such a voice to him from the excellent glory, This is my beloved Son, in whom I am well pleased. And this voice which came from heaven we heard, when we were with him in the holy mount. **We have also a more sure word of prophecy***; whereunto ye do well that ye take heed, as unto a light that shineth in a dark place, until the day dawn, and the day star arise in your hearts:* **Knowing this first, that no prophecy of the scripture is of any private interpretation. For the prophecy came not in old time by the will of man: but holy men of God spake as they were moved by the Holy Ghost***. But there were false prophets also among the people, even as there shall be false teachers among you, who privily shall bring in damnable heresies, even denying the Lord that bought them, and bring upon themselves swift destruction. And many shall follow their pernicious ways; by reason of whom the way of truth shall be evil spoken of. And* **through covetousness shall they with feigned words make merchandise of**

you: *whose judgment now of a long time lingereth not, and their damnation slumbereth not.*
(2 Peter 1:16–2:3, emphasis added)

Peter pointed out a couple of very interesting facts about prophecy in this passage. The first is that no prophecy is of private interpretation, meaning that all prophecy will agree with all other prophecy, and New Testament prophecy will be understood by the believer through his or her relationship with Christ. New Testament prophecy differs from what was given in the Old Testament because, under the new covenant, prophecy is spoken to believers who have the Holy Spirit dwelling inside of them; under the old covenant, prophets spoke by the unction of the Holy Spirit to people who did not have the Spirit of God dwelling within them. Old Testament believers had the law dictated to them, not written on their hearts; New Testament believers have God's law inscribed in their hearts and have been given the Holy Spirit within them to confirm it and guide them.

Any prophecy given to an individual under the new covenant must *bear witness* with the

Spirit dwelling in him. What has been said will be confirmed by the Spirit in his heart. Prophecy will be realized not by the person seeking to make it happen but simply through the believer continuing to follow God with all his heart, mind, soul, and strength. We should never pursue prophecy; we must always pursue Christ.

~

Any prophecy given to an individual under the new covenant must bear witness with the Spirit dwelling in him.

~

Many mistakes were made regarding prophecy in what has come to be known as the shepherding movement, where believers were encouraged to follow the "prophecies" and counsel of their leaders as if they were still under the old covenant.[26] These "prophecies" spoke of whom one should marry, business deals one should make, ministries one should embark upon, and other similar details, often with quite disastrous results. The mistake was that people pursued the

---

[26] It is worth noting here that David du Plessis was asked to take part in the initial 1975 meetings that helped right this "discipleship movement" and get its followers back onto a more correct course.

"prophecies" instead of God. When a prophecy turned out to be false, regardless of the sincerity of the person who delivered it, the hearer was led away from Christ instead of toward Him.

An example occurred in the life of David du Plessis when he first met Anna and the Lord told him she would one day be his wife. Although this was a specific word from the Lord, David did not act upon it by asking her to marry him the next day. Rather, he let things run their normal course and courted her for eighteen months before they married. He allowed the word of the Lord to be confirmed in him by following the wisdom of Scripture and not rushing things but instead practicing patience and preferring Anna above himself. As a result, their marriage lasted nearly sixty years.

Biblical Examples of Specific Prophecy

To cultivate an even deeper understanding of this, it is worth looking at three New Testament examples of prophecy given to individuals or groups. The first is Agabus' prophecy to Paul in Acts:

*And as we tarried there [in Caesarea] many
days, there came down from Judaea a certain prophet, named Agabus. And when he
was come unto us, he took Paul's girdle, and
bound his own hands and feet, and said,
Thus saith the Holy Ghost, So shall the Jews
at Jerusalem bind the man that owneth this
girdle, and shall deliver him into the hands
of the Gentiles.*

(Acts 21:10–11)

God sent Agabus to confirm what was already
in Paul's heart: that he was to go to Jerusalem to
be arrested, imprisoned, and eventually taken to
Rome to bear witness of Jesus. It is interesting to
note that those who heard the message with Paul
interpreted it as a warning that Paul was not to
go to Jerusalem, while Paul alone knew that it
was the course God was planning for him and
that Agabus' words were not only confirmation
of what lay ahead of him but also assurance that
it was God's will and that He would be with Paul
through it all. We see this later confirmed after
Paul is imprisoned in Jerusalem and the Lord
comes to speak to him:

> *And the night following the Lord stood by
> him, and said, Be of good cheer, Paul: for
> as thou hast testified of me in Jerusalem, so
> must thou bear witness also at Rome.*
>
> (Acts 23:11)

A second example of specific prophecy is the
words Christ spoke through John to the seven
churches of Asia in the first few chapters of the
book of Revelation. When you read these, you
very much see these prophecies edifying, exhort-
ing, or consoling. In each, the Lord speaks of
the church's strengths and then gives correction
and exhortation to return to first principles or
"correct course" back to what He has called it
to do. We also see consolation in each, ending
with Christ virtually throwing His arms open to
welcome them back in, or, as He so aptly put it
to the Laodiceans:

> *As many as I love, I rebuke and chasten:
> be zealous therefore, and repent. Behold, I
> stand at the door, and knock: if any man
> hear my voice, and open the door, I will
> come in to him, and will sup with him, and
> he with me. To him that overcometh will I
> grant to sit with me in my throne, even as*

I also overcame, and am set down with my Father in his throne. He that hath an ear, let him hear what the Spirit saith unto the churches.

(Revelation 3:19–22)

The third prophecy I would like to offer as an example is not actually included in the Scriptures, but it is referred to in Paul's letters to Timothy:

This charge I commit unto thee, son Timothy, according to the prophecies which went before on thee, that thou by them mightest war a good warfare; holding faith, and a good conscience; which some having put away concerning faith have made shipwreck ... Neglect not the gift that is in thee, which was given thee by prophecy, with the laying on of the hands of the presbytery. Meditate upon these things; give thyself wholly to them; that thy profiting may appear to all. Take heed unto thyself, and unto the doctrine; continue in them: for in doing this thou shalt both save thyself, and them that hear thee.

(1 Timothy 1:18–19; 4:14–16)

And Paul echoed again in his second letter to him:

> *Wherefore I put thee in remembrance that thou stir up the gift of God, which is in thee by the putting on of my hands. For God hath not given us the spirit of fear; but of power, and of love, and of a sound mind. Be not thou therefore ashamed of the testimony of our Lord, nor of me his prisoner: but be thou partaker of the afflictions of the gospel according to the power of God; who hath saved us, and called us with an holy calling, not according to our works, but according to his own purpose and grace.*
>
> (2 Timothy 1:6–9)

In these passages, we see that Paul's advice to Timothy is to *"meditate upon these things, give thyself wholly to them … Take heed to thyself, and unto doctrine, continue in them."* Thus, he asked him to meditate upon the prophecies spoken over him, aligning them with doctrine (for Timothy had no New Testament to refer to at this time), giving himself to these good things, while also "taking heed to himself," or measuring them by the Holy Spirit inside of him. If he did these things, then, according to Paul, he would save both himself and those who heard him. In the second letter, Paul also told him to stir up these gifts, finding courage from the spirit of power, love, and common sense within himself. Why? Because he had been called with a holy calling and enabled by God to bring it to pass. Was he to force these things to happen? No, he was to mediate on them, ponder them, and be ready to follow God into them as they were confirmed in his own heart through the Holy Spirit within him.

It is perhaps this last example that best parallels what David du Plessis experienced in Smith Wigglesworth's prophecy to him. First of all, it was given far in advance of its fulfillment so that David had plenty of time to think about it and ponder what it meant. Over the course of his meditation, God began to change attitudes in David's heart that needed to be changed before he became the man who could fulfill God's calling on his life. David also waited on God to open the doors and lead him before he began walking out the vision of what Smith had told him he would be doing with the majority of his life as a minister. He found himself taking gradual steps toward being the reconciler God had called him to be, first among the Pentecostals and then among all of the churches, even those so liberal they had become apostate. This leads to another major point about prophecy that David learned as God spoke to him and as he prayed and recovered in the hospital after his car accident: that prophecy is meaningless if it is not applied with love and forgiveness.

Prophecy Is Nothing Without Love

In the heart of his letter to the Corinthians in which he taught about spiritual gifts, Paul interjects the greatest discourse on the love of God found in the Bible. Of these Scriptures in 1 Corinthians 13, we tend to focus on verses 4–8, but look for a moment at what is written on either side of that famous passage:

> *And though I have the gift of prophecy, and understand all mysteries, and all knowledge; and though I have all faith, so that I could remove mountains, and have not charity [love], I am nothing... Charity [love] never faileth: but **whether there be prophecies,***

> ***they shall fail***; *whether there be tongues,*
> *they shall cease; whether there be knowledge,*
> *it shall vanish away. For we know in part,*
> *and we prophesy in part. But when that*
> *which is perfect is come, then that which is*
> *in part shall be done away.*

(1 Corinthians 13:2, 8–10, emphasis added)

Too often we are so fascinated by what is revealed in prophecy—in the power and wonder of truth uncovered—that we forget that if the truth is not applied in love, it is nothing. David's earliest instincts in hearing this Scripture were that he would march into ecumenical circles with the truth of God's Word and correct them as Jonah corrected the people of Nineveh. He was right, and they were wrong. He would go in and preach the truth, and they would fall to their knees, repenting in sackcloth and ashes, or be destroyed by the hand of the Lord. But, because of the cross, God no longer operates that way. The truth was to be offered in love, and in order to bring repentance, David first had to learn to offer forgiveness by forgiving those from the traditional denominations who had hurt him as a young Pentecostal.

Without love, prophecy will fail and come to an end, because we don't know it all—we see only in part and must walk out the rest by following the "God of love who is love."[27] Again, prophecy that creates pride is either false or misused; it is only prophecy that brings people closer to Christ and His love that is true.

In the Final Analysis

By considering these things, there is a great deal to be learned from the prophecy God gave through Smith Wigglesworth to David du Plessis and what God was hoping to see come of the Pentecostal/charismatic movements. God was not looking to create a new denomination but to reunify all believers in the bond of the Spirit. In many senses, it is easy to call this a failure, because, in the end, denominations divided further, creating a greater number; however, in a more important sense, it was a tremendous success. Through what has been sifted and separated into different movements—notably, what has been called the Pentecostal movement, the ecumenical movement, neo-Pentecostalism, and

---

[27] See 1 John 4:8, 16.

the charismatic renewal, the work has been done all by the same Spirit, and there is now a body of that Spirit within literally all the Christian denominations and paradenominations of the earth, which, according to the *World Christian Encyclopedia*, number nearly 34,000.[28]

The key to true unity is not becoming more like each other but each of us becoming more like Jesus, which is the primary work that the Holy Spirit does in anyone's life.

While "The Smith Wigglesworth Prophecy," as it has come to be known over time, has raised incredible interest because of the man who gave it and the revival it foretold, it is important to remember that it was not a prophecy for all of us. It was a prophetic word given specifically to David du Plessis so that he could ponder it, be changed by it, and, in the end, give himself wholly to it when it looked as if all of the rest of his brethren had forsaken him because of it. It is also important that the rest of us allow such men as David du Plessis to follow God when they are called to do so. It is an unfortunate mistake that his ordination papers were pulled by the

---

[28] Barrett et al., ed., *World Christian Encyclopedia*, 10.

Assemblies of God just as his ministry was peaking. And it is also unfortunate that Rev. du Plessis is not the only minister to whom this happened when he broke away from the mainstream to follow the voice of God.

Ordination is the recognition of God's call upon a life, not a means of trying to control someone and prevent any actions we may not fully support. It is good that the Assemblies of God later reinstated him, as has also happened with many others in similar circumstances, but it is nevertheless unfortunate that they were cast aside in the first place.

For a time, especially in the late 1950s and early 1960s, when David's ordination papers had been revoked, it was only David, God, and what God had spoken to him through Smith Wigglesworth. Of course, out of this, the important thing was that it was David and God, not David and the prophecy, for had he not continued to pursue God through it all—had he pursued the prophecy instead—it very well could have been the others who were right in pulling his papers, and not David.

However, the fact remains that this prophecy was specifically for David du Plessis—and it was fulfilled. Other prophecies, however—such as the one given to Tommy Hicks, which we will discuss in the Tommy Hicks book—were given more generally to the church and are still waiting for us to rise up and take part in their fulfillment.

Bibliography

Barrett, David B., ed. *World Christian Encyclopedia: A Comparative Survey of Churches and Religions in the Modern World,* 2nd ed., vol. 1. New York: Oxford University Press, 2001.

Burgess, Stanley M., and McGee, Gary B. ed. *Dictionary of Pentecostal and Charismatic Movements.* Grand Rapids, MI: Zondervan Publishing House, 1988.

"But What about Hicks?" *The Christian Century* (July 7, 1954): 814–815.

Durasoff, Steve. *Bright Wind of the Spirit: Pentecostalism Today.* Tulsa, OK: Rhema Bible Church, 1972.

Du Plessis, David (as told to Bob Slosser). *A Man Called Mr. Pentecost.* Plainfield, NJ: Logos International, 1977.

———. *Simple and Profound.* Orleans, MA: Paraclete Press, Inc., 1986.

———. *The Spirit Bade Me Go,* rev. ed. Plainfield, NJ: Logos International, 1970.

Frodsham, Stanley Howard. *Smith Wigglesworth: Apostle of Faith.* Springfield, MO: Gospel Publishing House, 1948.

Gibson, Houston. "Tommy Hicks Speaks at Denver Chapter," *Full Gospel Business Men's Voice* (November 1955): 27–29.

Hicks, Tommy (as recorded by Gerald Derstine). "Vision Given to Tommy Hicks, Evangelist, July 25, 1961." Reprinted from *Harvest Time* magazine, n.d.

———. *It's Closing Time, Gentlemen.* Los Angeles: Manifest Deliverance and Worldwide Evangelism, Inc., 1958.

————. *Millions Found Christ: History's Greatest Recorded Revival*. Los Angeles: Manifest Deliverance and Worldwide Evangelism, Inc., 1956.

————. "My Second World-Wide Mission Tour," *Full Gospel Business Men's Voice*, vol. 3, no. 7 (October 1955): 3–18.

Liardon, Roberts. *God's Generals: Why They Succeeded and Why Some Failed*. New Kensington, PA: Whitaker House, 1996.

Nickel, Thomas R. "A Subsequent Report of the Hicks Mission," *Full Gospel Business Men's Voice* (January 1956): 10–16.

Parham, Mrs. Charles. *The Life of Charles Parham*. Birmingham, AL: Commercial Printing Company, 1930.

Robinson, Martin. "To the Ends of the Earth: The Pilgrimage of an Ecumenical Pentecostal, David J. du Plessis (1905–1987)." Ph.D. dissertation: University of Birmingham, England, 1987.

Sandidge, Jerry L. "Roman Catholic/Pentecostal Dialogue: A Contribution to Christian Unity," *Pneuma* 7 (1985): 41–61.

Stokes, Louie W. The Great Revival in Buenos Aires. Buenos Aires, Argentina: 1954.

Wigglesworth, Smith. *Ever Increasing Faith*. Springfield, MO: Gospel Publishing House, 1924, 1971.

————. *Smith Wigglesworth Speaks to Students of the Bible*. Compiled by Roberts Liardon. Tulsa, OK: Albury Publishing, 1998.

————. *Smith Wigglesworth: The Complete Collection of His Life Teachings*. Compiled by Roberts Liardon. Tulsa, OK: Albury Publishing, 1996.

About the Compiler

Dr. Roberts Liardon is an author, public speaker, spiritual leader, church historian, and humanitarian. He was called into the ministry at a very young age, preaching his first public sermon at the age of thirteen and lecturing on God's Generals in Christian colleges and universities at age fifteen.

From age sixteen, he has utilized every platform to preach the Gospel of Jesus Christ, bring maturity to the Church, and encourage those in ministry. He has produced radio, television, and Internet programs, and has also authored over eighty books, which have been translated into over sixty languages and to date have sold 16.5 million copies.

Dr. Liardon has established many churches and accredited Bible schools. He is the senior leader of Embassy International Churches, headquartered in Orlando, Florida. He also founded and presides over the Embassy Global Network, which provides encouragement and counsel for ministries, churches, and leaders.

In great demand as a speaker and mentor to pastors and leaders worldwide, Dr. Liardon has ministered in over 127 nations and loves to pray, teach the Word of God, and prophesy to bless God's people. He speaks to a current generation of believers who want to draw closer to the heart and mind of God and impact their communities and the nations through the Gospel of Jesus Christ.

You may contact Dr. Liardon at:

www.robertsliardon.com
Facebook: Roberts Liardon Official
Twitter: Roberts Liardon
Instagram: robertsliardon_official
youtube.com/robertsliardon

U.S. Office:
Roberts Liardon Ministries
P. O. Box 781888
Orlando, FL 32878
Email: Admin@robertsliardon.org

UK and Europe Office:
Roberts Liardon Ministries
UK, 22 Notting Hill Gate, Suite 125
London W11 3JE, UK
Email: Admin@robertsliardon.org